God Loves Me
Bible

Susan Elizabeth Beck

ZONDERVAN.com/
AUTHORTRACKER
follow your favorite authors

God Loves Me Bible
Copyright © 2004 by The Zondervan Corporation

Requests for information should be addressed to:
Zonderkidz, *Grand Rapids, Michigan 49530*

Library of Congress Cataloging-in-Publication Data

Beck, Susan Elizabeth.
 God loves me Bible / by Susan Elizabeth Beck ; illustrated by Gloria
Oostema. – Rev. ed.
    p. cm.
  ISBN-10: 0-310-70779-X (hardcover)
  ISBN-13: 978-0-310-70779-0 (hardcover)
   1. Bible—Biography—Juvenile literature. 2. God—Love—Juvenile
literature. 3. Bible stories, English. I. Oostema, Gloria. II. Title.
  BS551.3.B43 2004
  220.9'505–dc22

2004007669

Editor: Catherine DeVries
Art direction: Laura Maitner
Interior design: Laura Maitner
Editor of original edition: Jean E. Syswerda

Printed in China

13 / LPC / 19 18 17 16 15 14 13

The

Beginning

Creation

Genesis 1

In the beginning there was nothing.
Then God made the sky and the earth.

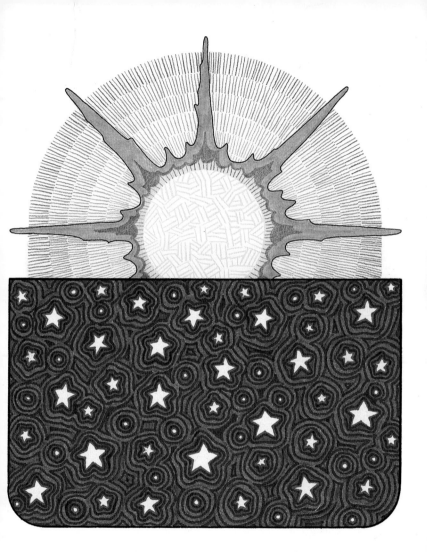

God made the sun and the stars.

God made the water and the land.
He made the fish and the
birds and all the animals.
He put them on the earth.

God loved his world.

And God loves me!

Adam and Eve

Genesis 2

God made two people
to take care of his world.
He made a man named
Adam and a woman
named Eve. Adam and Eve
lived in a beautiful place
called the Garden of Eden.

God loved Adam and Eve.

And God loves me!

Noah

Genesis 6–8

Noah was God's friend. God told Noah to build a big boat because a flood was coming. Noah listened to God. He built the boat. Then he put his family in the boat and many animals too. When the terrible flood came, Noah and his family and the animals were safe inside the boat.

God loved Noah and his
family and the animals.

And God loves me!

God loved

the world,
Adam and Eve,
Noah and his family,
and the animals.

Do you know who
else God loves?

Me!

More
People
on the Earth

Abraham

Genesis 12; 15

God chose Abraham to be the
father of a special nation of
people. God promised
Abraham as many children as
there are stars in the sky.

God loved Abraham.

And God loves me!

Sarah

Genesis 18; 21

Sarah was very, very old. God told her she would have a baby. Sarah laughed. An old lady couldn't have a baby! But God gave Sarah and Abraham a son. They named him Isaac.

God loved Sarah.

And God loves me!

Isaac

Genesis 22

Isaac was Abraham and Sarah's
only child. As a test, God told Abraham
to sacrifice Isaac. Abraham was very,
very sad. But he was willing to obey
God. Abraham passed God's test.
God sent a ram and Abraham
sacrificed it instead. God promised to
make their family into a great nation.

God loved Isaac.

And God loves me!

Rebekah

Genesis 24–25

Rebekah was a very beautiful girl.
She was kind and she was brave.
Rebekah left her family and moved
far away. She married Isaac, and Isaac
loved her. Rebekah became the mother
of twin boys: Jacob and Esau.

God loved Rebekah.

And God loves me!

Jacob

Genesis 28

Jacob had a dream. He saw a stairway going up to heaven. Angels were walking up and down the stairway. God stood at the very top. God spoke to Jacob. He promised Jacob a lot of land and many children. God promised never to leave Jacob.

God loved Jacob.

And God loves me!

Rachel

Genesis 29–30; 35

Rachel was a beautiful girl.
She took care of her father's sheep.
She married Jacob, and he loved her.
Rachel had two sons:
Joseph and Benjamin.

God loved Rachel.

And God loves me!

Joseph

Genesis 37

Joseph's father loved him very much.
He gave Joseph a colorful robe.
But Joseph's brothers didn't like him.
They sent Joseph far from home.
But God kept Joseph safe. He made
Joseph a great man in Egypt.

God loved Joseph.

And God loves me!

God loved

Abraham and Sarah,
Isaac and Rebekah,
Jacob and Rachel,
Joseph, and all the
people he had created.

Do you know who
else God loves?

Me!

God's Special People:
The
Israelites

The
Baby
Moses

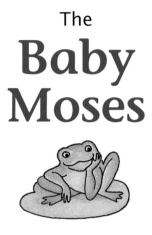

Exodus 2

Moses' mother was a slave in Egypt. She hid him from the soldiers. The soldiers were trying to hurt Moses and other Hebrew baby boys. She put baby Moses in a basket and placed it in the Nile River. A princess found Moses. She kept him safe from the soldiers.

God loved baby Moses.

And God loves me!

The
Leader
Moses

Exodus 3

Moses talked with God.
God spoke to Moses from
a burning bush. God told
Moses to help his people the
Israelites. Moses became a
great leader of God's people.

God loved the leader Moses.

And God loves me!

The
Israelite
Slaves

Exodus 1; 7–12

God's people lived in Egypt.
They worked very hard for the king.
They were unhappy, so they prayed to
God. God sent Moses to ask the king
to let the people go. But the king said,
"No!" Then God sent terrible plagues—
frogs and grasshoppers and boils
and flies. There were ten in all.
Then the king let God's people go.

God loved the Israelite slaves.

And God loves me!

Miriam

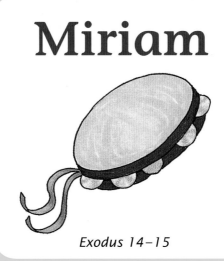

Exodus 14–15

Miriam was Moses' sister. She left
Egypt with him and all God's people.
God parted the waters of the Red
Sea so they could walk across on
dry land. When Miriam reached the
other side, she danced and sang
a special song of thanks to God.

God loved Miriam.

And God loves me!

The
Hungry
Israelites

Exodus 16

God's people took a long trip in
the desert. They became very
hungry. God sent special bread
from heaven every morning to
cover the ground. The people
called the bread manna.

God loved his people the Israelites.

And God loves me!

Moses

Climbs a Mountain

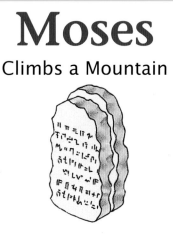

Exodus 19–20

God told Moses to climb a
mountain. Moses was up there
for a long time. God gave Moses
ten rules for the people to follow.
Moses called these rules the
Ten Commandments.

God loved Moses.

And God loves me!

Caleb and Joshua

Numbers 13

Twelve men went to explore the promised land of Canaan. Ten of the men were scared and said God's people should not go there. But Caleb and Joshua thought the land was wonderful. They knew God would help his people conquer Canaan.

God loved Caleb and Joshua.

And God loves me!

Joshua

Joshua 5–6

Joshua was a great leader. He led God's people to the promised land. Joshua's army conquered the city of Jericho. God told them to march around the city. He told them to shout and blow trumpets. Then God made the walls of Jericho fall down.

God loved Joshua.

And God loves me!

God loved

Moses and Miriam
and Caleb
and Joshua
and God's
special people,
the Israelites.

Do you know who
else God loves?

God's People in the

Promised
Land

Deborah

Judges 4–5

Deborah was a prophet and a
judge. She trusted God.
She helped people stop fighting.
When an enemy came to attack,
Deborah showed Barak and his
army how to defeat them. God's
people won! Deborah wrote a
beautiful song of thanks to God.

God loved Deborah.

And God loves me!

Samson

Judges 13–16

Samson was strong, and he
was special. When Samson was
young, he obeyed God. But when
he grew up, he did not always
obey God. But God still used
Samson as a leader of God's people.

God loved Samson.

And God loves me!

Ruth

Ruth 1–4

Ruth was sad. Her husband had died.
She had no children, but she loved
her husband's mother Naomi. Ruth
promised never to leave Naomi. She
promised to love Naomi's God and
her people. God blessed Ruth. He
gave her a new husband and a son.

God loved Ruth.

And God loves me!

Samuel

1 Samuel 3

When Samuel was a little boy, he lived in the temple. One night he heard a voice calling his name— one, two, three times. When the voice called again, Samuel said, "Here I am, LORD." Samuel listened to God. He obeyed God all of his life.

God loved Samuel.

And God loves me!

God loved

Deborah and Samson
and Ruth and Samuel
and all God's people
in the promised land.

Do you know who
else God loves?

The
Kings

Saul

1 Samuel 10

Saul was taller than the other men
in Israel. But Saul was shy. He hid
when the people wanted to make
him king. But the people found him.
They put a crown on his head, and
they made Saul the first king of Israel.

God loved Saul.

And God loves me!

The Shepherd Boy
David

1 Samuel 16–17

David was a shepherd. He took good care of his father's sheep. He was strong and brave. When a lion and a bear attacked the sheep, David saved the sheep.

God loved the shepherd boy David.

And God loves me!

The Fighter
David

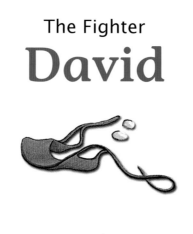

1 Samuel 16–17

David was too young to join the army. But one day he fought the enemy all alone! He fought a giant named Goliath. David was much smaller than Goliath, and Goliath called him names. But David trusted God, and he won!

God loved the fighter David.

And God loves me!

King David

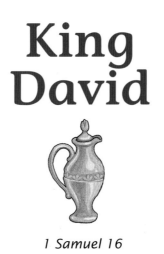

1 Samuel 16

David was the youngest boy in
his family. No one thought he could
be a king. But God chose David to
be a great and powerful king.

God loved King David.

And God loves me!

Jonathan

1 Samuel 20

Jonathan was the son of King Saul.
Jonathan was best friends with David.
He shot arrows with David in the
fields. Jonathan protected David
when King Saul was angry.

God loved Jonathan.

And God loves me!

Solomon

1 Kings 3; 6

Solomon was a good and fair king of Israel. He asked God to make him wise. God gave Solomon his wish. God also made Solomon very rich. Solomon built a beautiful temple for God in Jerusalem.

God loved Solomon.

And God loves me!

Joash

2 Kings 12

Joash was the king of Judah. He wanted to make God's temple a beautiful place again. The people gave Joash a lot of money to pay for the work. Joash gave the money to the workers who fixed up God's temple. Joash was a good king.

God loved Joash.

And God loves me!

Josiah

2 Kings 22

Josiah was a little boy when he became king of Israel. He was only eight years old! One day the priests found some very old books in the temple. Josiah told the priests to read the books to the people. The people loved to hear what God said in the books.

God loved Josiah.

And God loves me!

God loved

Saul and David and
Jonathan and Solomon
and all the kings
of his nation.

Do you know who
else God loves?

Me!

The
Prophets

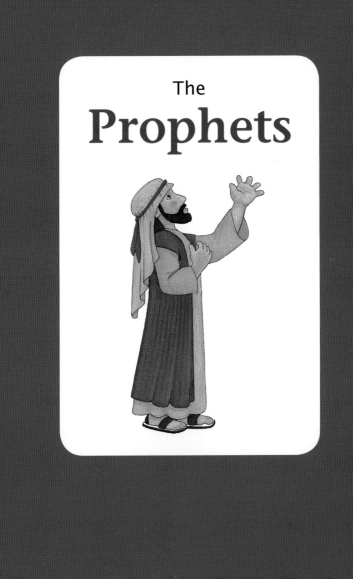

The Prophet
Elijah

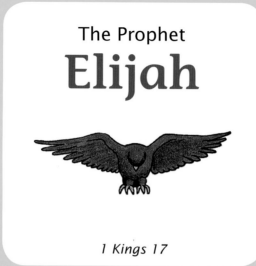

1 Kings 17

Elijah loved God and obeyed him.
When there was no food to eat, God
sent birds to bring food to Elijah.

God loved the prophet Elijah.

And God loves me!

Elijah
Goes to Heaven

2 Kings 2

One day Elijah took a walk with his friend Elisha. Suddenly a chariot and horses of fire flew between Elijah and Elisha. Then a whirlwind came and picked Elijah up and carried him to heaven.

God loved Elijah.

And God loves me!

Isaiah

Isaiah 6

God needed someone to bring news
to his people the Israelites. God asked
Isaiah to be his messenger. At first,
Isaiah was afraid. He didn't think he
could do the job. But then he said,
"Here I am. Send me." Isaiah became
a great messenger of God to
the Israelites.

God loved Isaiah.

And God loves me!

Jonah

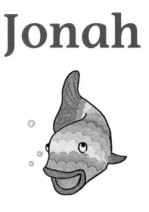

Jonah 1–4

God told Jonah to go to Nineveh.
But Jonah didn't listen. He got
on a ship and sailed away. When
a storm came, Jonah was thrown
into the sea. A big fish swallowed
Jonah. Jonah prayed to God,
and God saved him.

God loved Jonah.

And God loves me!

God loved

Elijah and Isaiah
and Jonah
and all his messengers.

Do you know who
else God loves?

Me!

God's People
Away From Home

Shadrach, Meshach, Abednego

Daniel 3

Shadrach, Meshach, and Abednego were taken far away to a country called Babylon. The king wanted them to worship a golden idol. But the three men loved God. They would not worship anything else. So the king threw them into a fire. It was very, very hot. But the three men did not get burned. God kept them safe.

God loved Shadrach,
Meshach, and Abednego.

And God loves me!

Daniel

Daniel 6

Every day Daniel prayed to God. One
day the king said, "No one may pray
to God." But Daniel prayed anyway.
The king ordered the soldiers to throw
Daniel into a den of lions. But God kept
Daniel safe. The lions did not hurt
him. Daniel trusted and obeyed God.

God loved Daniel.

And God loves me!

Esther

Esther 2–9

Esther became the queen of a great
nation. A wicked man made a plan
to kill all of the Israelites. When
Esther found out about the plan,
she told the king. Esther trusted
God, and God's people were saved.

God loved Esther.

And God loves me!

Ezra

Ezra 7–8

Ezra lived in Babylon. He was a
teacher. He studied God's rules.
One day the king told him he could
go back home to Israel. Ezra led
many, many people back to the city
of Jerusalem. With the help of the
people, Ezra rebuilt God's temple.

God loved Ezra.

And God loves me!

God loved

Daniel and Esther
and Ezra
and all God's people
who were far
away from home.

Do you know who
else God loves?

Jesus

Comes to Earth

Mary

Luke 1

Mary was a young girl who loved God. One day an angel came to Mary. The angel told Mary she would have a baby boy. The baby would be God's Son, and his name would be Jesus. Mary was a wonderful mother.

God loved Mary.

And God loves me!

Joseph

Matthew 1

Joseph was a carpenter. He loved
Mary very much, and he planned to
marry her. An angel told Joseph that
Mary was going to have a baby—
God's Son. Joseph took good care
of Mary and the baby Jesus.

God loved Joseph.

And God loves me!

The
Baby Jesus

Matthew 2; Luke 2

Jesus was a very special baby. He was born in a stable in Bethlehem. Angels appeared to the shepherds and told them Jesus was born. A very bright star sparkled in the sky. The Wise Men followed the star from far away to see Jesus and bring him gifts. Jesus was the Son of God.

God loved the baby Jesus.

And God loves me!

The
Boy Jesus

Luke 2

Jesus was 12 years old when he went to the temple in Jerusalem with Mary and Joseph. When it was time to go home, Jesus stayed in the temple. He listened to the teachers there and asked many questions. All the people were amazed at how smart Jesus was.

God loved the boy Jesus.

And God loves me!

John the Baptist

Matthew 3

John the Baptist was a preacher. He lived in the desert. His clothes were made of camel hair, and he ate bugs and honey. John told the people that Jesus was coming to save them from their sins. John baptized many people in the Jordan River.

God loved John the Baptist.

And God loves me!

God's Son Jesus

Matthew 3

Jesus came to John the Baptist to
be baptized in the Jordan River.
When Jesus came out of the river,
a dove landed on his shoulder.
A voice from heaven said,
"This is my Son, and I love him."

God loved his Son Jesus.

And God loves me!

God loved

Mary and Joseph, John the Baptist,
and Jesus—when he was a baby,
when he was a little boy,
and when he was grown up.

Do you know who
else God loves?

Jesus

Teaches the People

The 12
Disciples

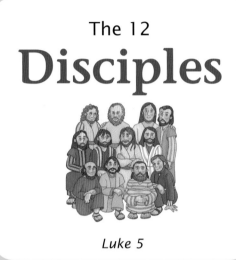

Luke 5

Jesus had 12 special friends.
They were called his disciples.
The disciples were ordinary
people. Jesus chose them
to tell others about God.

God loved the 12 disciples.

And God loves me!

A Very Sick
Little Girl

Luke 8

Jairus had a little daughter. She was
very sick. Jairus went to Jesus for help.
Jesus came to their house. Everyone
was crying because the little girl
was dead. Then Jesus did something
wonderful! He took the little girl by
the hand and made her alive again!

God loved the little girl.

And God loves me!

Mary and Martha

Luke 10

Mary and Martha were friends of Jesus. One day Martha got angry because Mary listened to Jesus instead of helping in the kitchen. But Jesus told Martha that Mary had chosen the right thing.

God loved Mary and Martha.

And God loves me!

The
Little
Children

Mark 10

Some people brought their children to see Jesus. They wanted Jesus to touch them and pray for them. The little children were very special to Jesus. He talked to them. He gave them hugs!

God loved the little children.

And God loves me!

Zacchaeus

Luke 19

Zacchaeus was a very short man.
He climbed a tree so he could see
Jesus as he walked by. Jesus
stopped to talk to Zacchaeus.
Then Jesus ate supper with him.

God loved Zacchaeus.

And God loves me!

The
Risen Jesus

John 19–20

Jesus knew God sent him to
earth to die for everyone's sins.
But Jesus did not stay dead.
He came out of his grave three
days later, just like he said he would!

God loved his Son Jesus.

And God loves me!

Jesus

Goes to Heaven

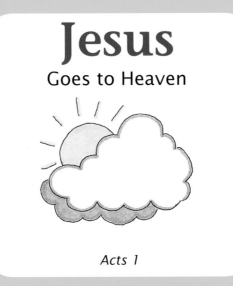

Acts 1

After Jesus rose from the dead, he taught his disciples many more good things. Then Jesus went up into heaven. He disappeared behind a cloud. His disciples were all alone. Two angels appeared. They promised that Jesus would come to earth again!

God loved his Son Jesus.

And God loves me!

God loved

Mary and Martha
and Zacchaeus and all the
people Jesus knew on earth.

Do you know who
else God loves?

Me!

Yes, God loves me!

The Beginning

More People on the Earth

God's Special People: The Israelites

God's People in the Promised Land

The Kings

ZONDERVAN.com/
AUTHORTRACKER
follow your favorite authors

We want to hear from you. Please send your comments about this book to us in care of zreview@zondervan.com. Thank you.

Grand Rapids, MI 49530
www.zonderkidz.com